COLLECTIVE SOUL

GUITAR ANTHOLOGY SERIES

Cover Art:

HINTS, ALLEGATIONS AND THINGS LEFT UNSAID
© 1993 Atlantic Recording Corporation

DISCIPLINED BREAKDOWN
© 1997 Atlantic Recording Corporation

COLLECTIVE SOUL
© 1995 Atlantic Recording Corporation

DOSAGE
© 1999 Atlantic Recording Corporation

Project Managers: AARON STANG & COLGAN BRYAN
Project Coordinator: SHARON MARLOW
Cover Design: JOSEPH KLUCAR

WARNER BROS. PUBLICATIONS - THE GLOBAL LEADER IN PRINT
USA: 15800 NW 48th Avenue, Miami, FL 33014

WARNER/CHAPPELL MUSIC
CANADA: 15800 N.W. 48th AVENUE
MIAMI, FLORIDA 33014
SCANDINAVIA: P.O. BOX 533, VENDEVAGEN 85 B
S-182 15, DANDERYD, SWEDEN
AUSTRALIA: P.O. BOX 353
3 TALAVERA ROAD, NORTH RYDE N.S.W. 2113
ASIA: UNIT 901 - LIPPO SUN PLAZA
28 CANTON ROAD
TSIM SHA TSUI, KOWLOON, HONG KONG

NUOVA CARISCH
ITALY: VIA CAMPANIA, 12
20098 S. GIULIANO MILANESE (MI)
ZONA INDUSTRIALE SESTO ULTERIANO
SPAIN: MAGALLANES, 25
29015 MADRID
FRANCE: CARISCH MUSICOM,
25, RUE D'HAUTEVILLE, 75010 PARIS

IMP
INTERNATIONAL MUSIC PUBLICATIONS LIMITED
ENGLAND: GRIFFIN HOUSE,
161 HAMMERSMITH ROAD, LONDON W6 8BS
GERMANY: MARSTALLSTR. 8, D-80539 MUNCHEN
DENMARK: DAMMUSIK, VOGNMAGERGADE 7
DK 1120 KOBENHAVNK

CONTENTS

BLAME

Words and Music by
ED ROLAND

Gtr. 1 is tuned to "open D"
and Capo III:
⑥=D ③=F#
⑤=A ②=A
④=D ①=D

Tempo I (Slowly ♩ = 74)
Intro:

*Capo III, sounding key is F.

Blame - 7 - 1

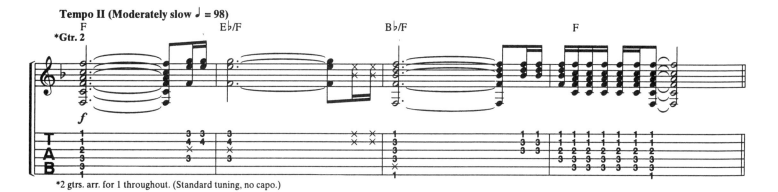

*2 gtrs. arr. for 1 throughout. (Standard tuning, no capo.)

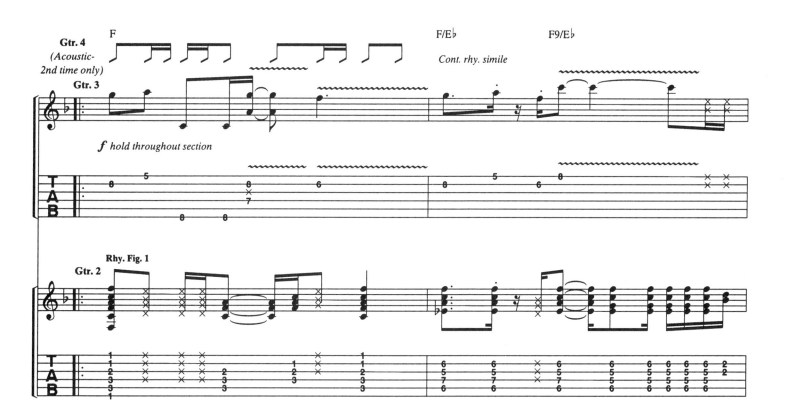

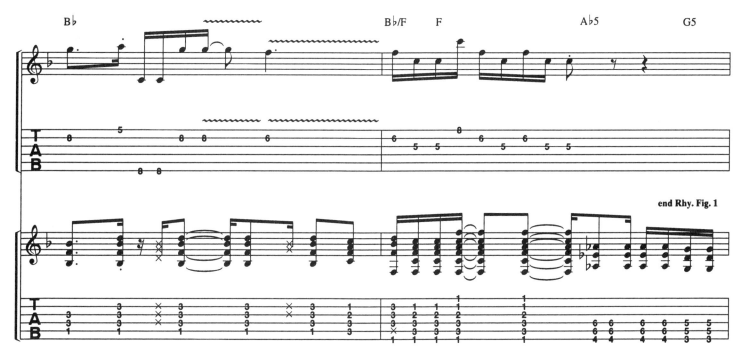

6

8

9

Blame - 7 - 6

10

demp - tion's— now of - fered.—

Tempo I
Outro:

Verse 2:
You lay me out
In hopes that I'd wilt away.
But strength rained down
And love provided shade.
(To Pre-Chorus 2:)

Pre-Chorus 2:
So while the pageant of lies
Still glows from your tongue,
Don't blame me for your Kingdom Come.
(To Chorus:)

DANDY LIFE

Words and Music by
ROSS CHILDRESS

12

that we say, but I try to an-y-way, ___ an-y-how. ___

born yes-ter-day 'cause I nev-er thought of things quite in that way at all, ___

___ and in that way.{ For what's in a day ___ of a dan-dy life, for

what's in a day ___ of this dan-dy life? Ev-'ry-thing, ___ ev-'ry-thing, ev-'ry-thing.

Chorus:

Rhy. Fig. 2

Gtr. 4
mf

(Ooh. _____)

Hang-ing on ___ ev-'ry word. ___

Gtr. 2
(right)

Gtr. 5

Rhy. Fig. 2A

f *w/dist.*

hold throughout
mf

Gtr. 3
(left)

Gtr. 6

Rhy. Fig. 2B

f *w/dist.*

mf *w/Leslie cabinet effect*

w/Rhy. **Figs. 2** *(Gtr. 4)*, **2A** *(Gtr. 5)* & **2B** *(Gtr. 6)* each 3 times

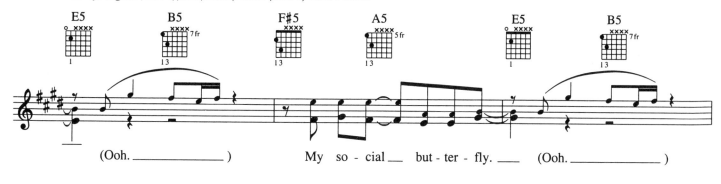

(Ooh. _____)   My so - cial __ but - ter - fly. ___   (Ooh. _____)

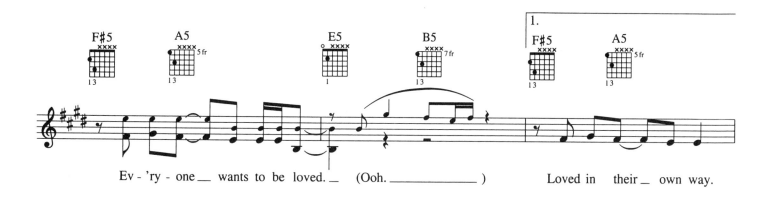

Ev - 'ry - one __ wants to be loved. __   (Ooh. _____)   Loved in their __ own way.

w/Rhy. **Fig. 1** *(Gtr. 1)*

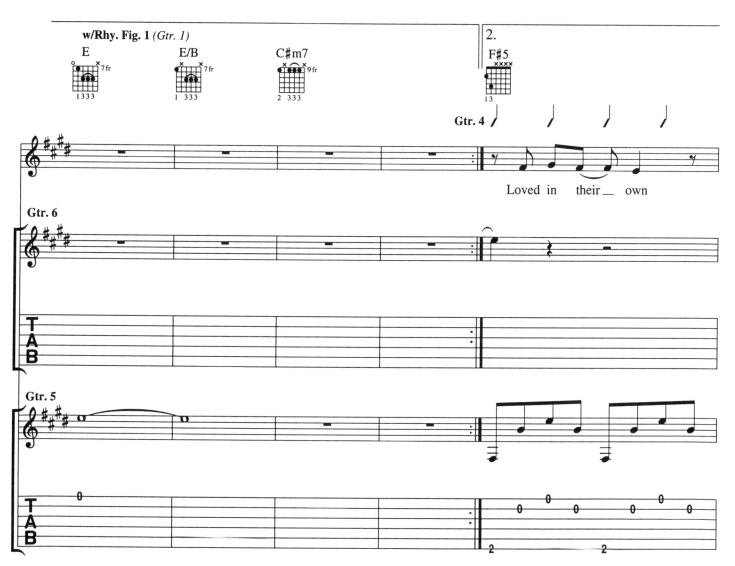

Loved in their __ own

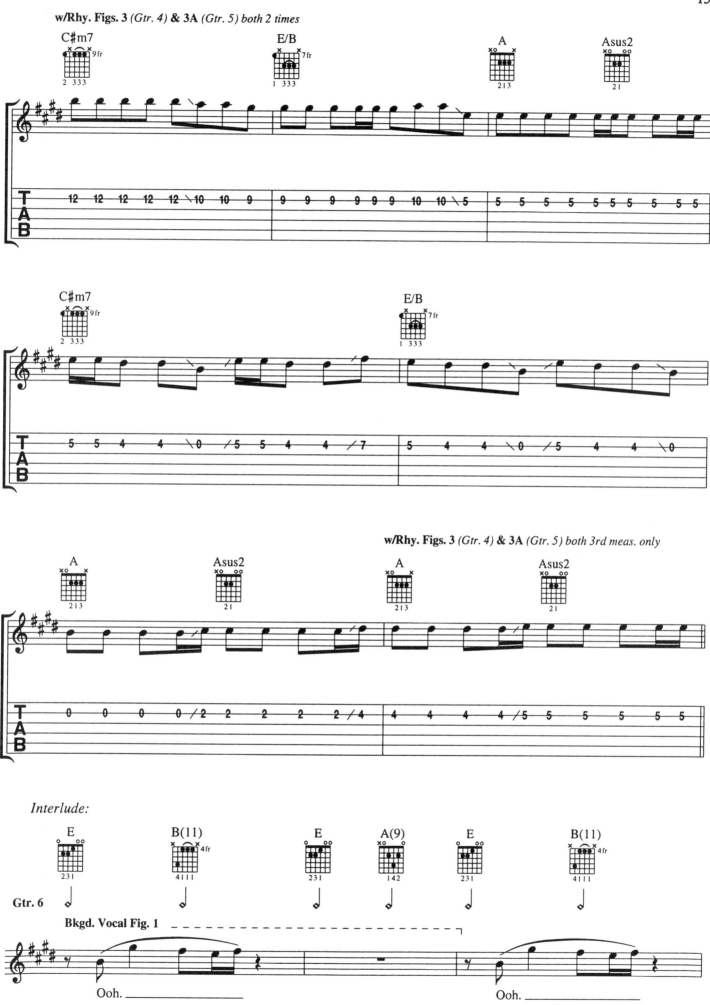

Chorus:

w/Rhy. Figs. 2 *(Gtr. 4),* **2A** *(Gtr. 5)* **& 2B** *(Gtr. 6) each 7 times*
w/Bkgd. Vocal Fig. 1, *8 times*

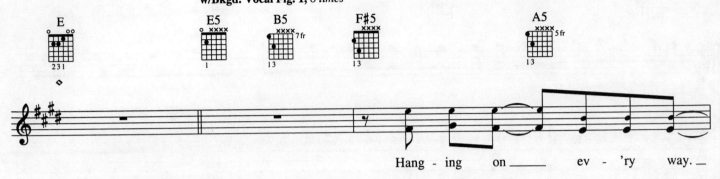

Hang - ing on ____ ev - 'ry way. ____

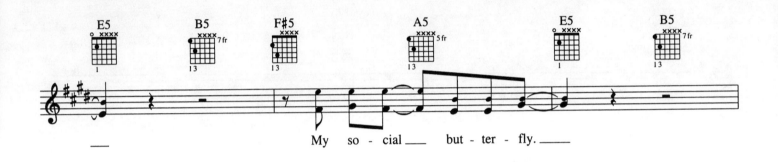

____ My so - cial ____ but - ter - fly. ____

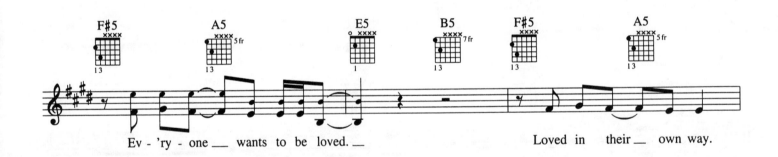

Ev - 'ry - one ____ wants to be loved. ____ Loved in their ____ own way.

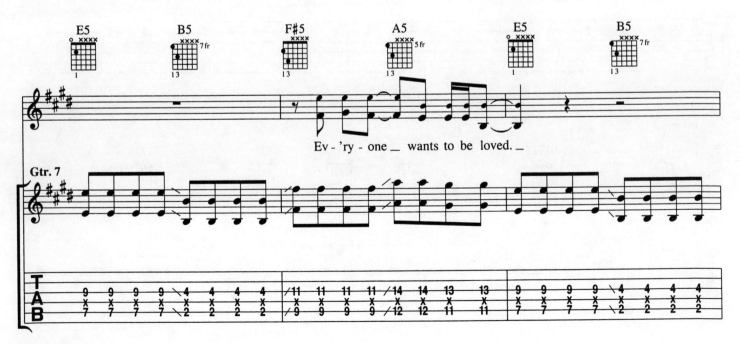

Ev - 'ry - one ____ wants to be loved. ____

Gtr. 7

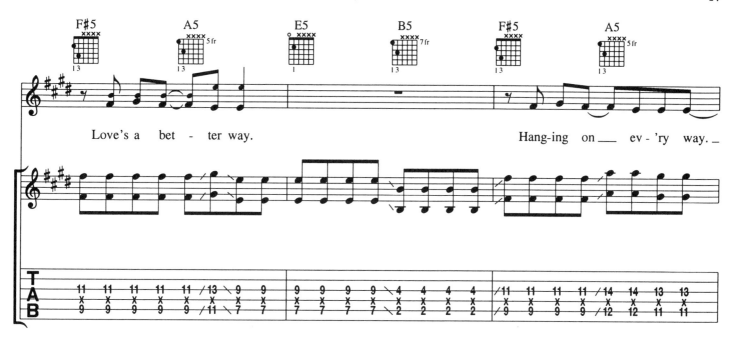

Love's a bet - ter way.

Hang-ing on ___ ev - 'ry way. __

w/Rhy. Fig. 2B *(Gtr. 6)*

Gtr. 4

Gtr. 7

Gtr. 5

DECEMBER

Music and Lyrics by
ED ROLAND

20

by, just spit me out.___ Don't wor - ry 'bout, don't speak of doubt.

Turn your head, now ba - by, just spit me out.___

Ooo___

DISCIPLINED BREAKDOWN

Words and Music by
ED ROLAND

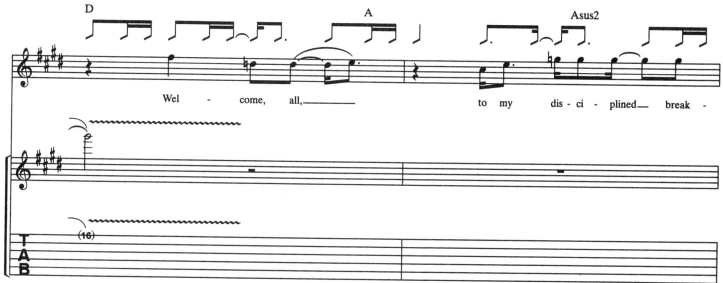

Wel - come, all, _____ to my dis - ci - plined _ break -

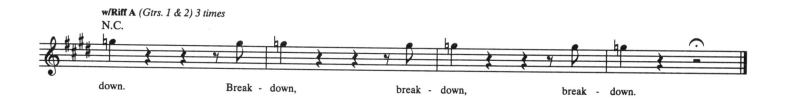

w/Riff A *(Gtrs. 1 & 2) 3 times*
N.C.

down.   Break - down,   break - down,   break - down.

Verse 2:
I never, ever can decipher who listens to the words I say.
While I sense I'm searching, I never know who's lurking
To scare my sacred thoughts away.
I'd love to hang and chat awhile,
But my mind's become vile.
(To Chorus:)

Verse 3:
I never, ever can contribute to finding all the faults that sustain,
Never mind the answers to who spreads the cancer,
When the questioning of why remains.
I'd love to sit and rationalize, but my tongue's become dry.
(To Chorus:)

GEL

Music and Lyrics by
ED ROLAND

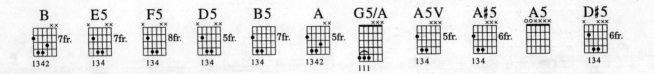

*Applies to both gtrs.

Gel - 8 - 1

30

32

*Chords derived from overall tonality.

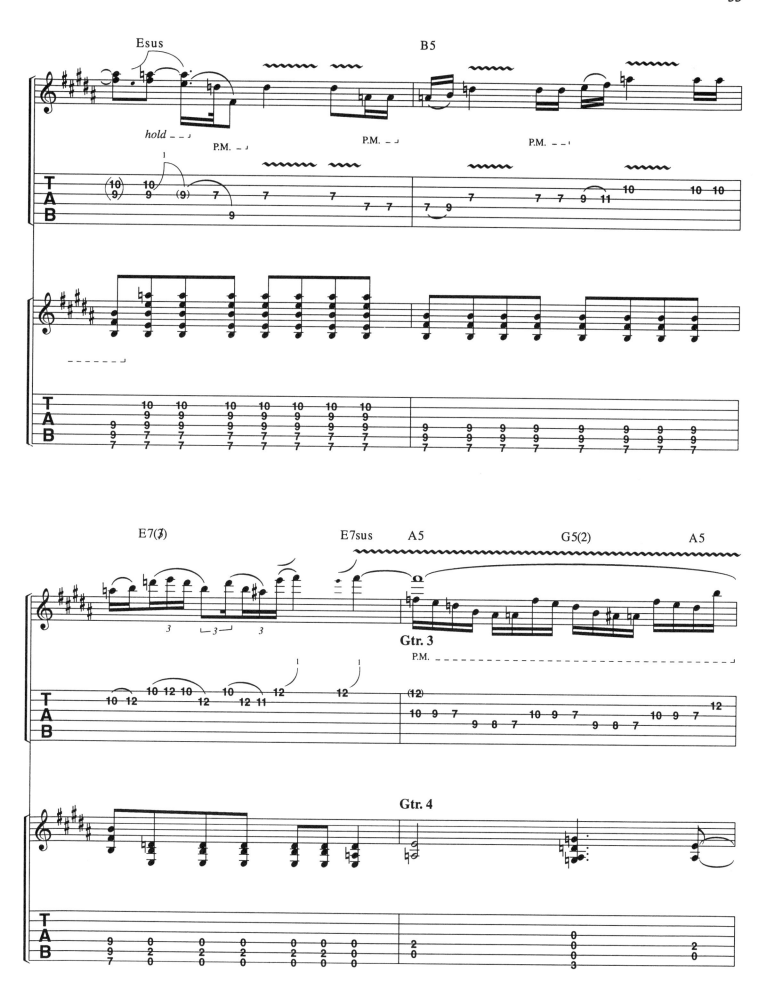

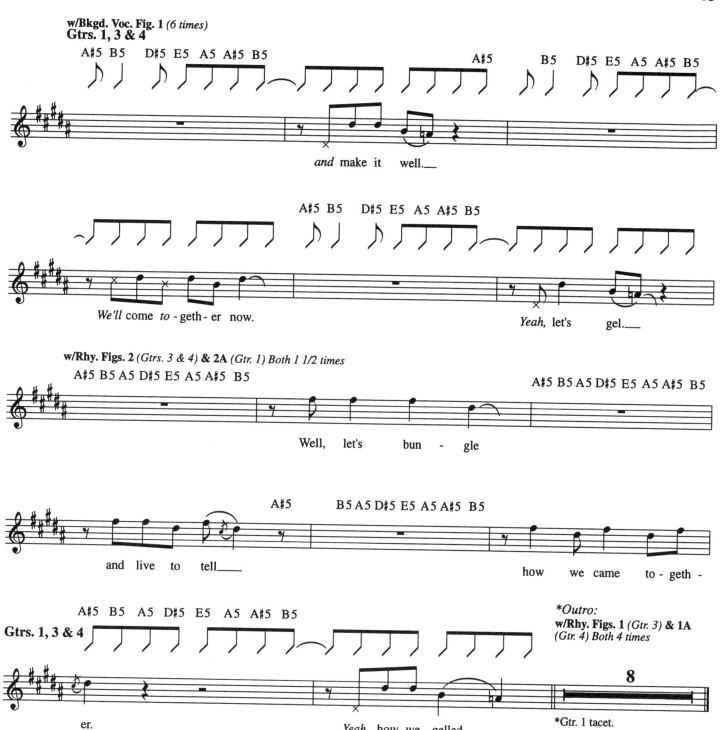

Verse 2:
Clothe me in any fashion.
Glitter to so mundane.
Tell me how you'd love to change me.
Tell me I can stay the same.
Well, I just want to shake us up.
Well, I just want, I just-a want to,
To shake us up.
(To Chorus:)

GIVING

Words and Music by
ED ROLAND

1. Giv-ing me cause so I may yearn, giv-ing me words so I may learn, and

2.3. *See additional lyrics*

I want more, I want more.

Giv-ing me thoughts that I may keep, giv-ing me dreams so I may sleep, and

Giving - 2 - 1

Verse 2:
You're giving me calm to fall into,
Giving me hope to guide me through,
And I want more, I want more.
Giving me light to see through tears,
Giving me strength to crash my fears,
And I want more, I want more.
Still, all I need is love,
So give me more.
(To Chorus:)

Verse 3:
You're giving me choice so I may seek,
Giving me faith so I'll believe,
And I want more, I want more.
Giving me breath of your mercy,
Giving yourself to comfort me,
And I want more, I want more.
Still, all I need is love,
So give me more.
(To Outro:)

GOODNIGHT, GOOD GUY

Words and Music by
ED ROLAND

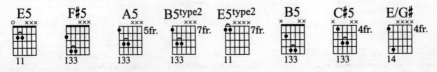

Moderately ♩ = 106
Intro:
N.C.
Elec. Gtrs. 1 & 2 (w/dist.)

Composite arrangement.

Cont. in slashes

Verse:

1. Some-bod-y told me a-bout a worn out dis-trac-tion that I had let slip a way.
2. I'll break the bread of a new day and won-der if faith will car-ry me a-long.

Goodnight, Good Guy - 7 - 1

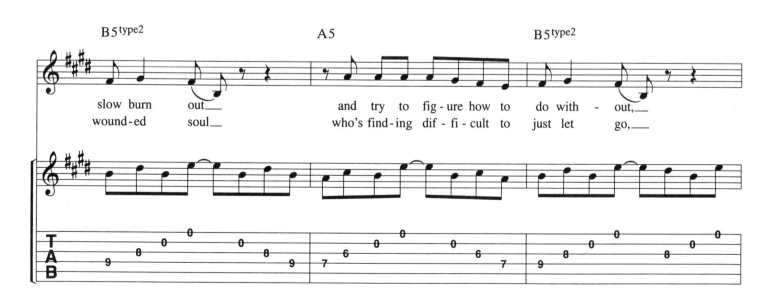

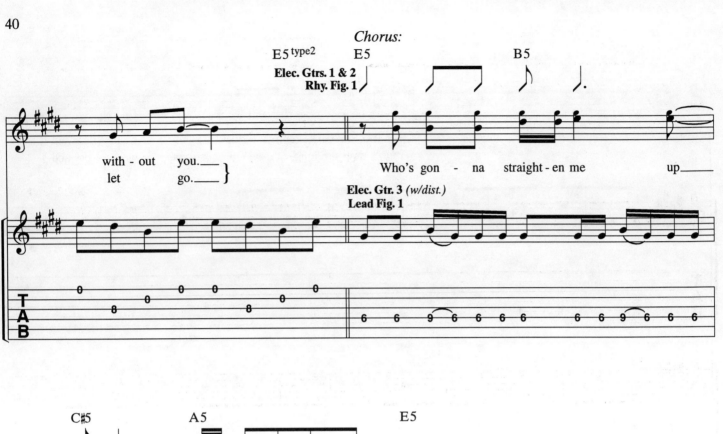

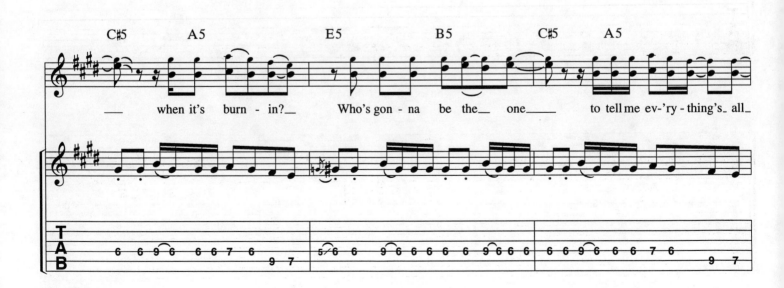

42

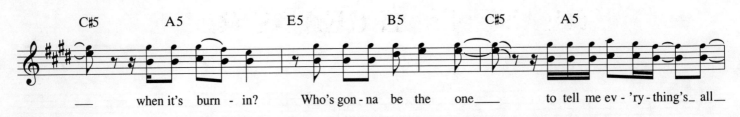

when it's burn - in? Who's gon - na be the one___ to tell me ev - 'ry - thing's_ all

___ right? Well,___ good-night. ___ good-night, good guy.___

Outro:
N.C.

Elec. Gtrs. 1 & 2

HEAVEN'S ALREADY HERE

Words and Music by
ED ROLAND

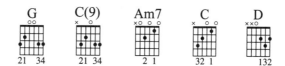

Acous. Gtr. 2 Capo V

Moderately ♩ = 88

Intro:

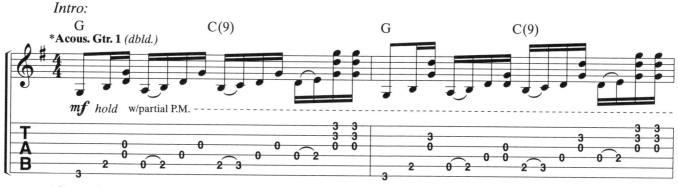

*Composite arrangement.

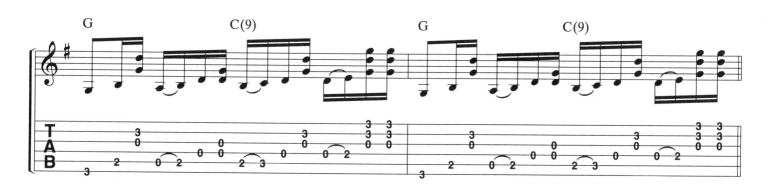

Verse:

1. Wake up to___ a new morn - ing,
2. No more liv - ing in dark - ness,

Elec. Gtr. (clean tone on repeat)

Heaven's Already Here - 3 - 1

*Transposed for capo at 5th fret.

HEAVY

All gtrs. tune down 1/2 step:
⑥ - Eb   ③ - Gb
⑤ - Ab   ② - Bb
④ - Db   ① - Eb

Words and Music by
ED ROLAND

Moderate rock ♩ 104

Intro:

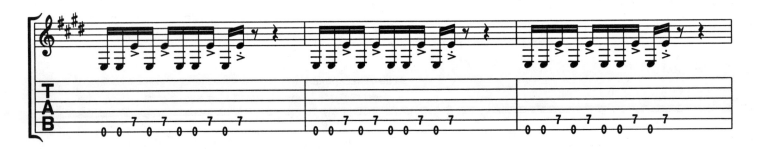

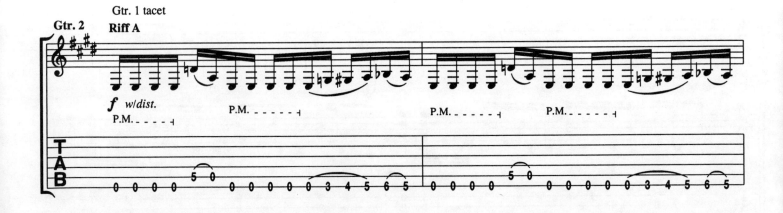

Heavy – 7 – 1

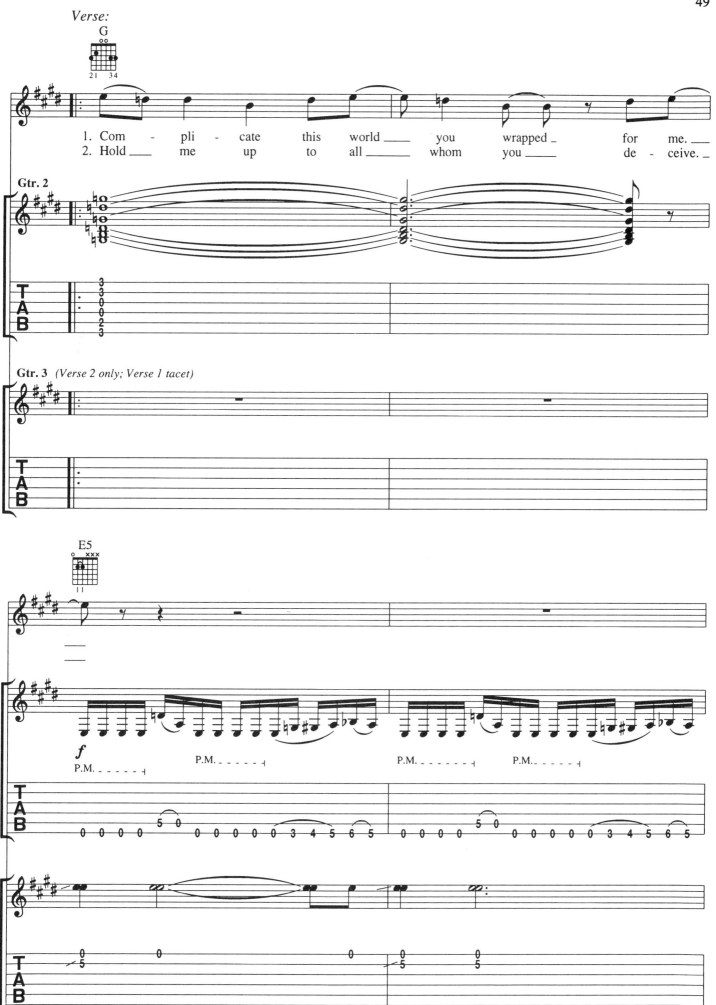

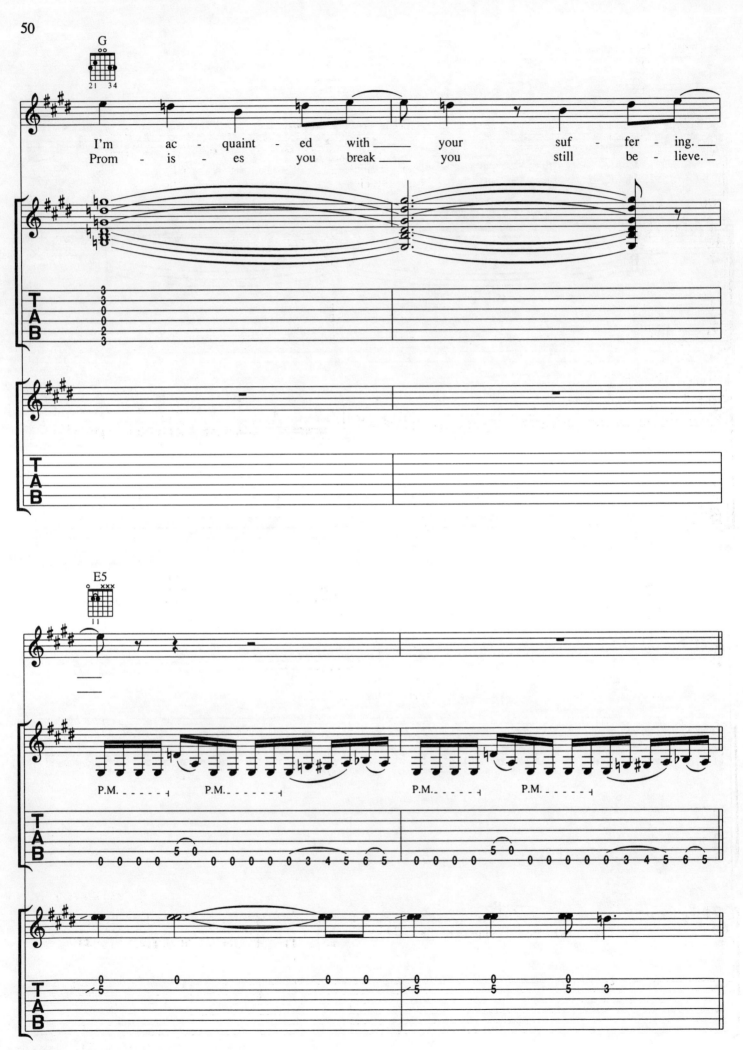

*Bass plays F#.

52

Heavy – 7 – 5

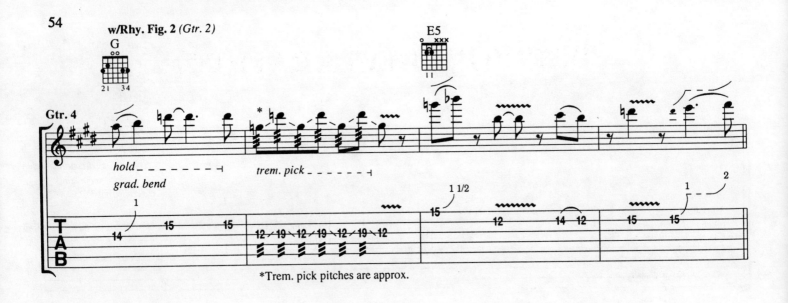

*Trem. pick pitches are approx.

Chorus:

And all your weight, _____ it falls on me, _____ it brings me down. _

_____ And all your weight, _____ it falls on me, _____ it falls on me. _

Outro:

PRECIOUS DECLARATION

Words and Music by
ED ROLAND

Precious Declaration - 5 - 1

56

Precious Declaration - 5 - 2

58

59

Verse 2:
New meanings to the words I feed upon
Wake within my veins
Elements of freedom.

Pre-Chorus 2:
Whoo, can't break now,
Yeah, I've been living for this.
Whoo, won't break now.
I'm cleansed with hopefulness.
(To Chorus:)

REUNION

Music and Lyrics by
ED ROLAND

Reunion - 4 - 1

*Gtr. 2 in G tuning: ⑥ = D ⑤ = G ④ = D ③ = G ② = B ① = D

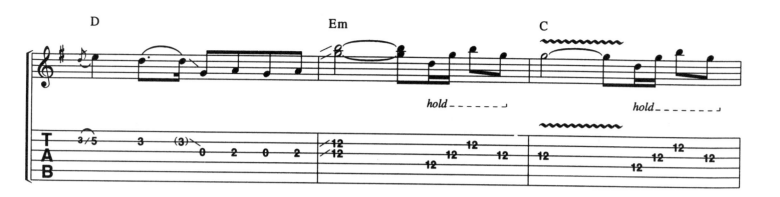

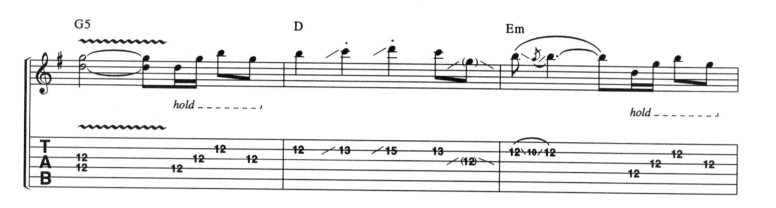

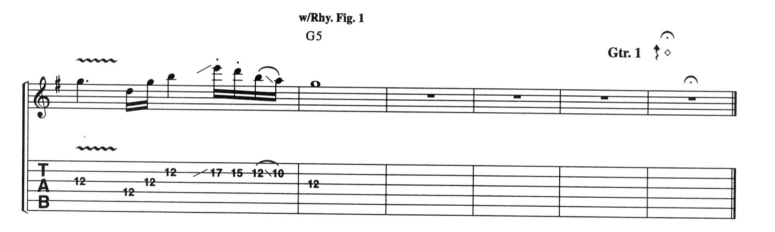

Verse 2:
Change has been.
Change will be.
Time will tell,
Then time will ease.
Now my curtain has been drawn.
And my heart can go
Where my heart does belong.
I'm going home.
(To Guitar Solo:)

RUN

Words and Music by
ED ROLAND

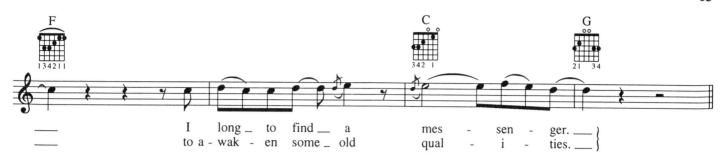

I long _ to find _ a mes - sen - ger. _ }
to a - wak - en some _ old qual - i - ties. _ }

Chorus:

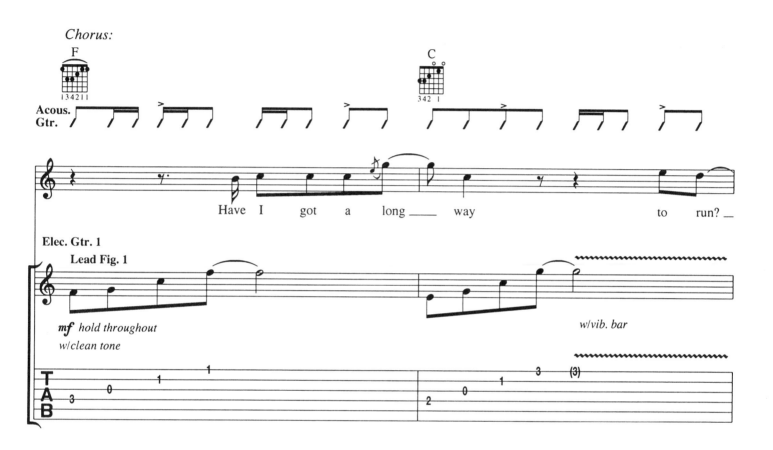

Have I got a long _____ way to run? _

Elec. Gtr. 1

Lead Fig. 1

mf hold throughout
w/clean tone

w/vib. bar

end Lead Fig. 1

Run – 5 – 2

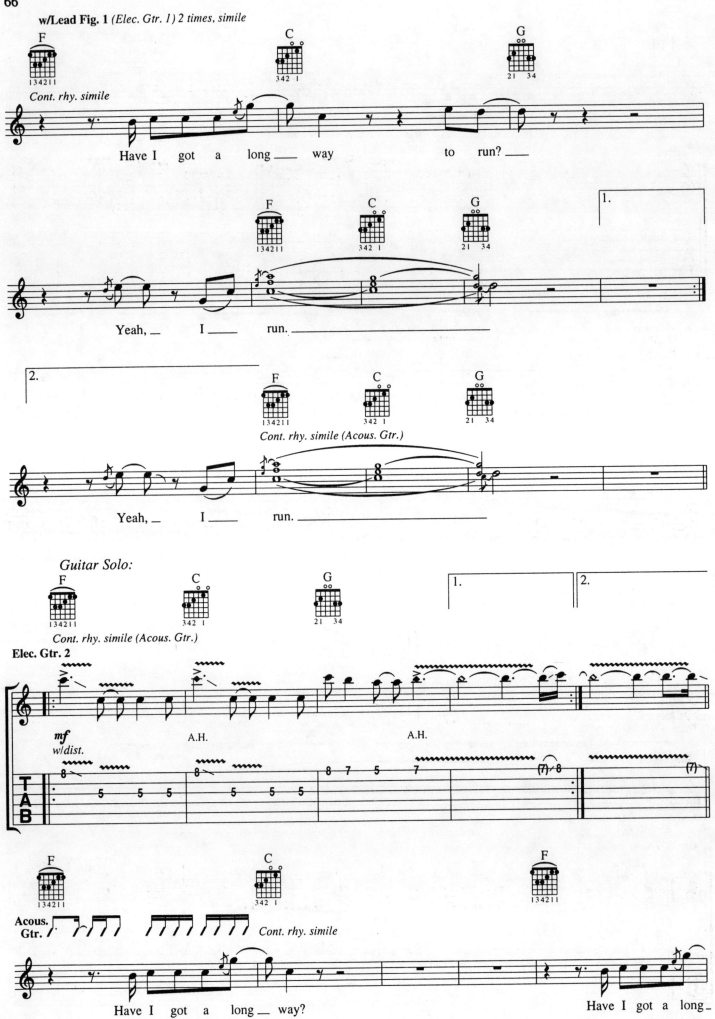

68

Run – 5 – 5

SHE SAID

All gtrs. tune down 1/2 step:
⑥= Eb ③= Gb
⑤= Ab ②= Bb
④= Db ①= Eb

Words and Music by
ED ROLAND

Moderately ♩ = 90

Intro:

She said that time is un-fair (a) to a wom-an her age. And now that wis-dom has

come, ev-'ry-thing else ____ fades.

She said she re-al-iz-es she's seen her bet-ter days. ___

She Said – 7 – 1

She said her dad - dy ___ had dreams, ___ but he drank them ___ a - way.
She said she won't speak ___ of love, ___ 'cause love she nev - er known.

And her moth - er's to blame for the way she is to - day.
And it's mo - ments like these, she hates to be a - lone.

72

3.She said she's still search -

for - give (a) me?" _ Mm, (a) she said. _

Guitar Solo:

SHINE

Words and Music by
ED ROLAND

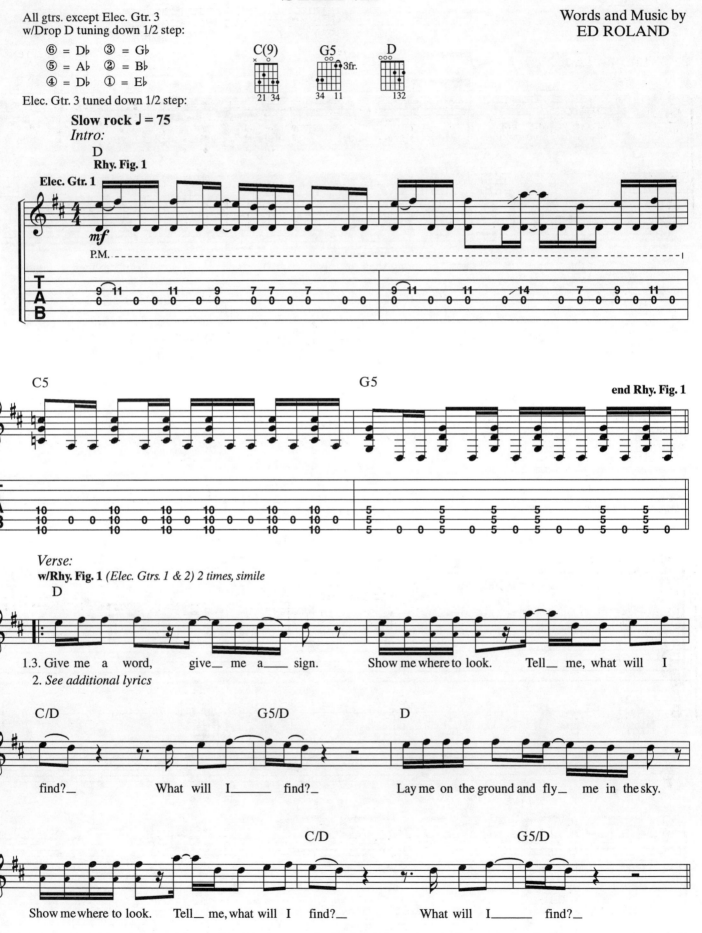

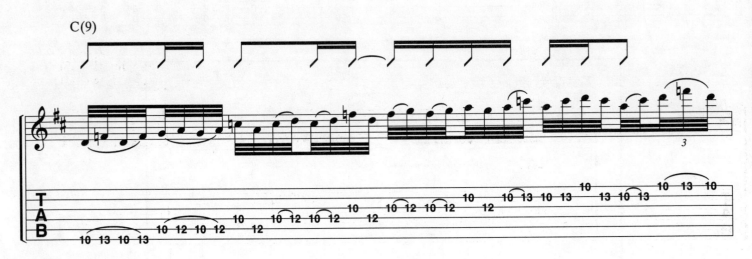

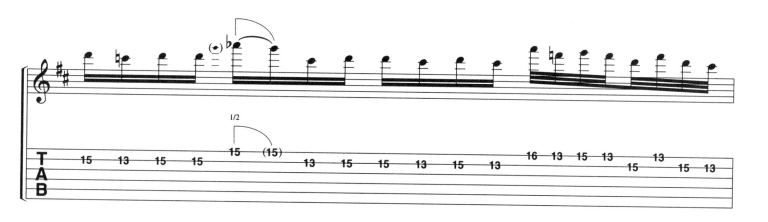

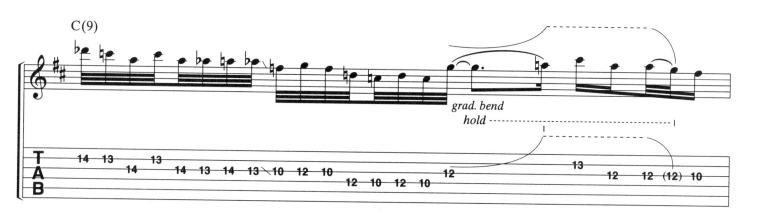

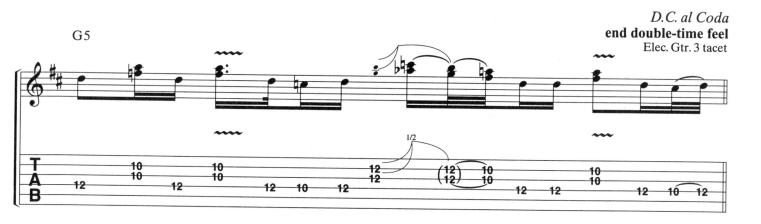

Shine - 5 - 4

Verse 2:
Love is in the water,
Love is in the air.
Show me where to look.
Tell me, will love be there?
Will love be there?

Teach me how to speak,
Teach me how to share.
Teach me where to go.
Tell me, will love be there?
Will love be there?
(To Pre-chorus:)

SIMPLE

Music by ED ROLAND & ROSS CHILDRESS
Lyrics by ED ROLAND

Simple - 9 - 1

82

Verses 1 & 2:
w/Riff A *(Gtrs. 1 & 2, 2 times)* **& Rhy. Fig. 2** *(Gtr. 3, 4 times)*

1. Tan - gle up your twist - ed tongue.___ It's sim - ple.
2. *See additional lyrics*

*Gtr. 4 play Verse 2 only.

Mes - mer - ize___ your ev' - ry - day.___ It's sim - ple.

w/Rhy. Fill 1 *(Gtr. 4, 4 times, Verse 2 only)*

Hey,___ hey, can't you see? Love is all___ that you should need.

Gtrs. 1 & 2

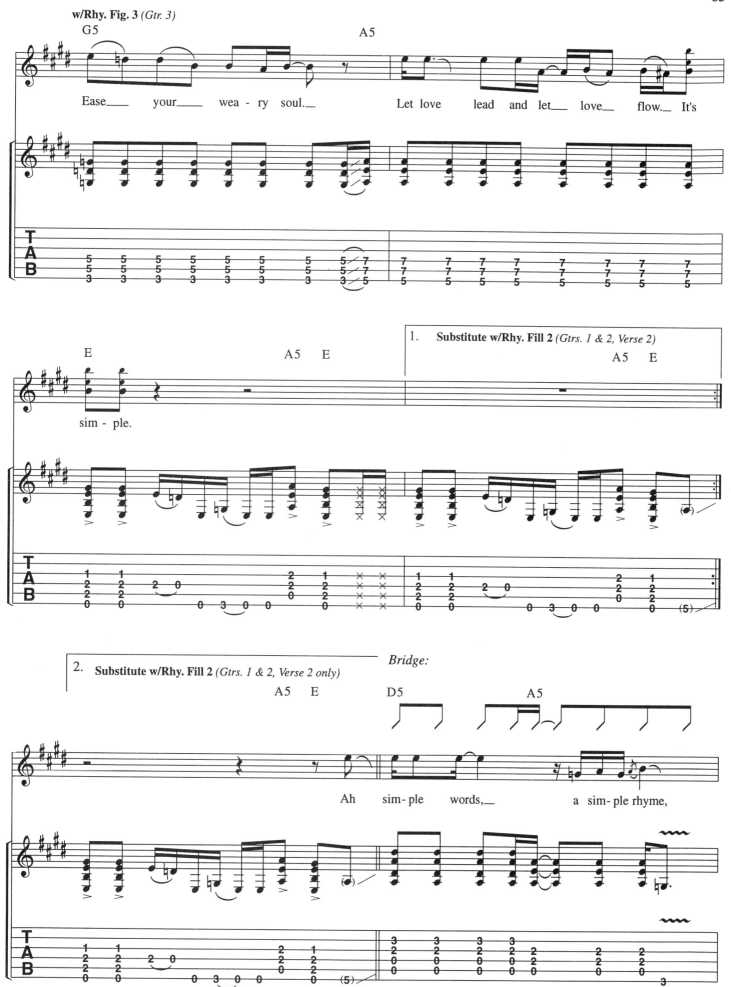

86

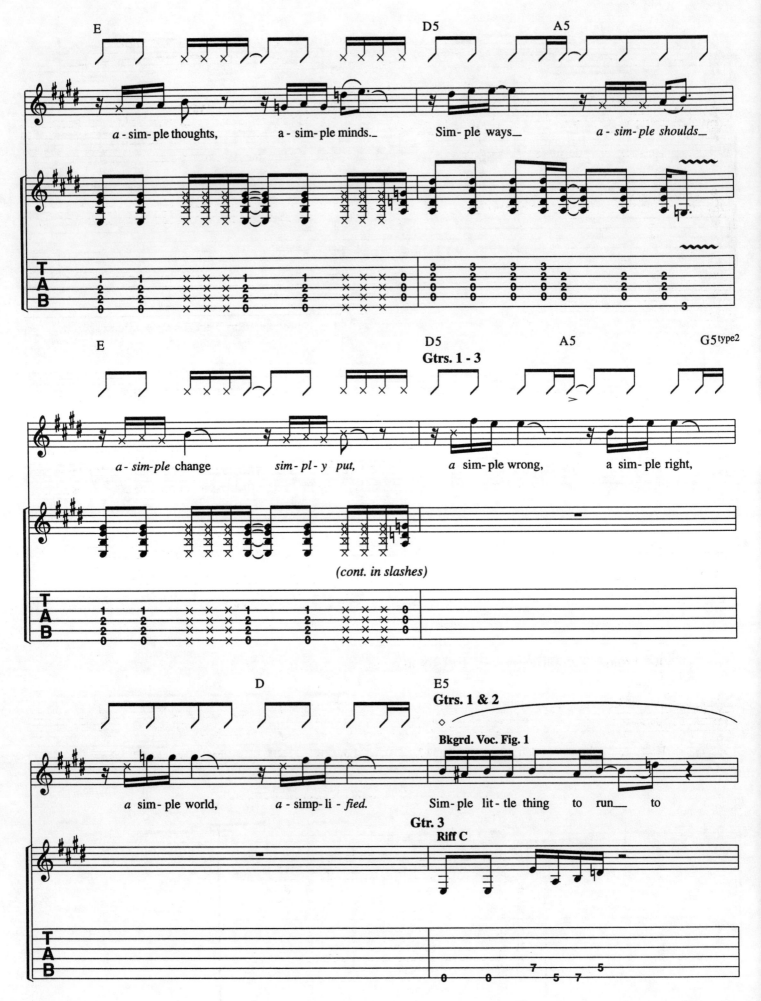

w/Rhy. Figs. 4 *(Gtrs. 1 & 2, 10 times)* **& 4A** *(Gtr. 3, 10 times)*

Want a sim - ple lit - tle thing to push___

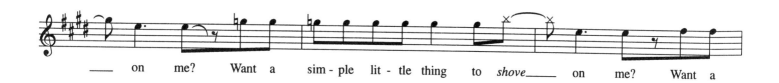

___ on me? Want a sim - ple lit - tle thing to *shove*___ on me? Want a

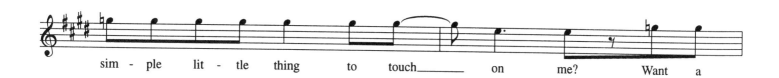

sim - ple lit - tle thing to touch___ on me? Want a

sim - ple lit - tle thing to love___ on me? *Yeah!*

Gtr. 4   **Riff D** - - - - - - -

f   *pick sl.*   *grad. bend*

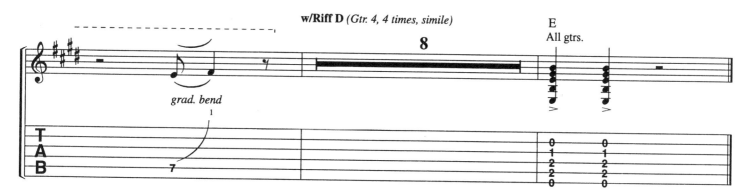

w/Riff D *(Gtr. 4, 4 times, simile)*   E   All gtrs.

grad. bend

Verse 2:
Pry into combative times. It's simple.
Forfeit all your lush concerns. It's simple.
Hey, hey, don't you care?
Love is all that you should share.
Hey, hey, don't you care?
(To Chorus:)

TREMBLE FOR MY BELOVED

Words and Music by
ED ROLAND

Tremble for My Beloved – 6 – 1

* Rock wah pedal with an eighth-note rhythm pattern.

Tremble for My Beloved – 6 – 2

92

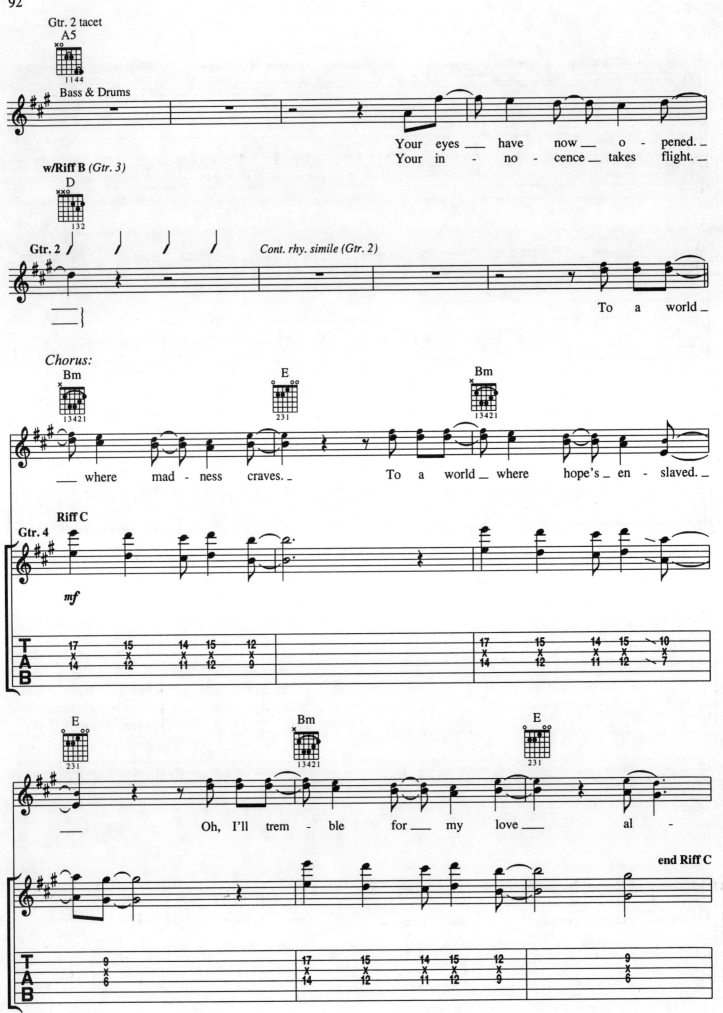

ways.

2. Your win - dow's o - pened wide. __

ways.

Guitar Solo:

* Rock wah pedal with an eighth-note rhythm pattern.

Chorus:
w/Riff C (Gtr. 4)

___ where mad - ness craves. ___ It's a world ___ where hope's en - slaved. ___

___ Oh, I trem - ble for ___ my love ___ al -

Tremble for My Beloved – 6 – 6

WHERE THE RIVER FLOWS

Music and Lyrics by
ED ROLAND

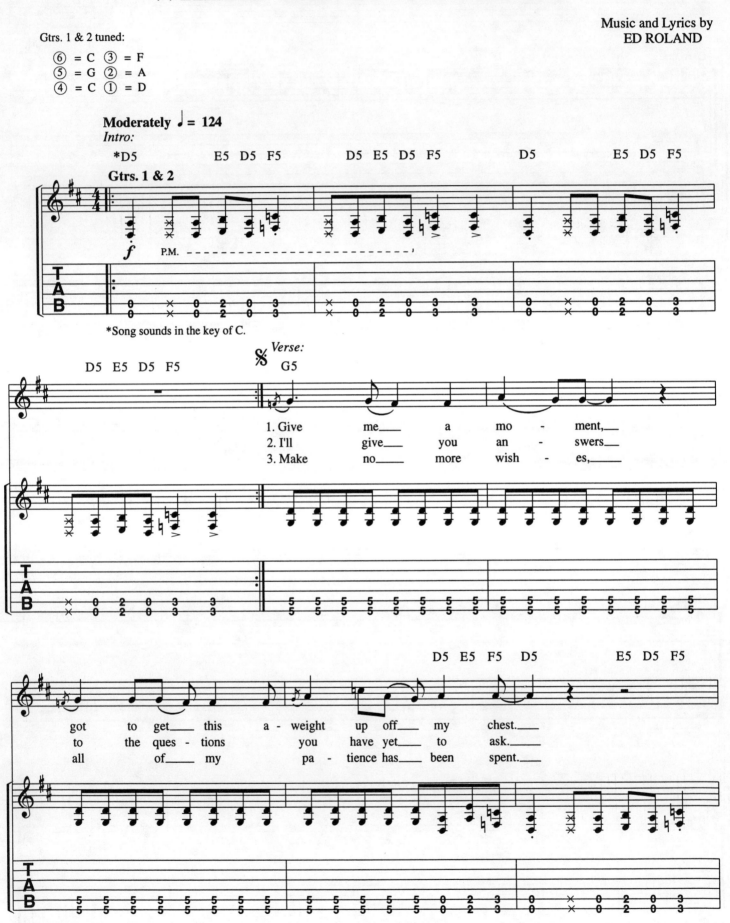

Where The River Flows - 6 - 1

D.S. 𝄋 al Coda

D5   E5 D5 F5   D5   E5 D5 F5   D5   E5 D5 F5   D5   E5 D5 F5

Both gtrs.

Coda   A5   D5   G5

Find your-self___ a - noth - er soul___ to   hold._____   You

flows.

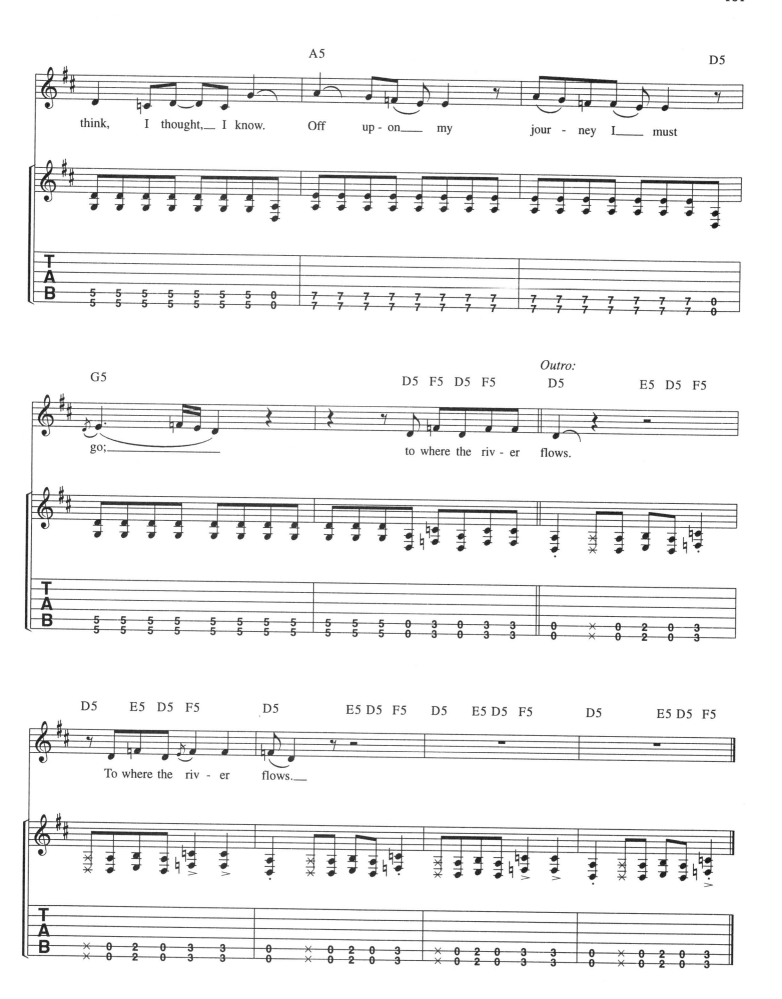

SISTER DON'T CRY

Words and Music by
ED ROLAND

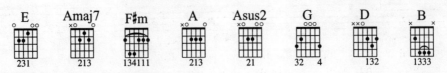

Moderately slow ♩ = 80

Intro:

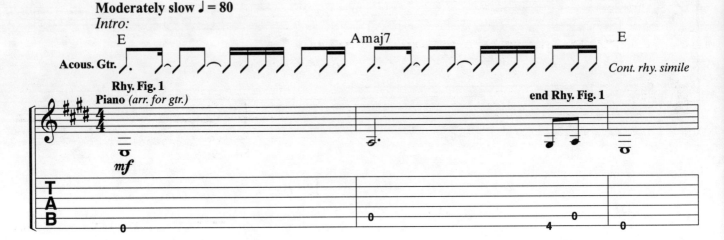

Verse:
w/Rhy. Fig. 1 *(Piano)* 4 times, simile

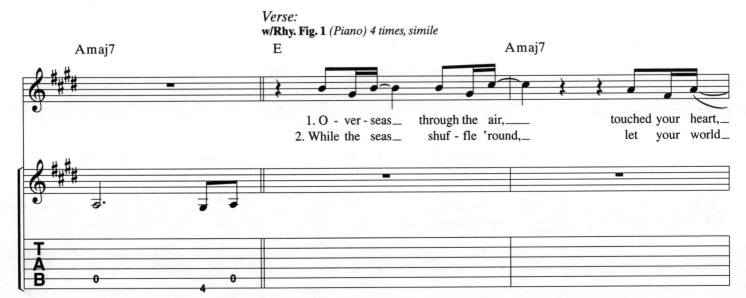

1. O - ver - seas___ through the air,___ touched your heart,___
2. While the seas___ shuf - fle 'round,___ let your world___

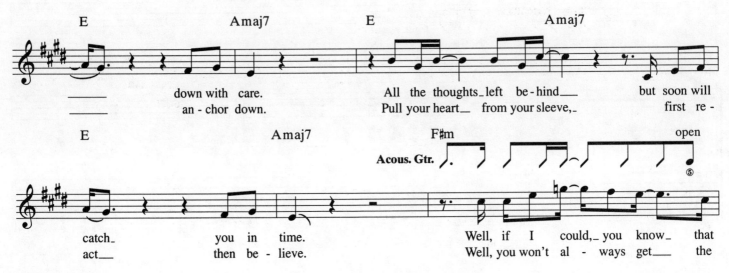

___ down with care. All the thoughts___ left be - hind___ but soon will
___ an - chor down. Pull your heart___ from your sleeve,___ first re -

catch___ you in time. Well, if I could,___ you know___ that
act___ then be - lieve. Well, you won't al - ways get___ the

Sister Don't Cry - 3 - 1

104

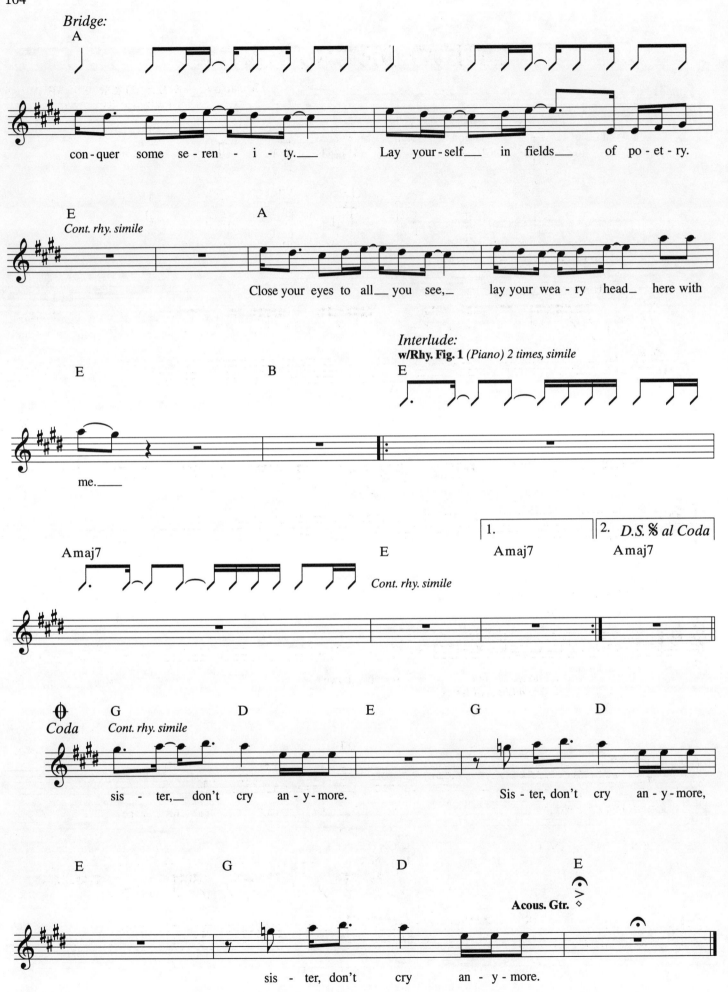

THE WORLD I KNOW

Music by ED ROLAND & ROSS CHILDRESS
Lyrics by ED ROLAND

The World I Know - 5 - 1

108

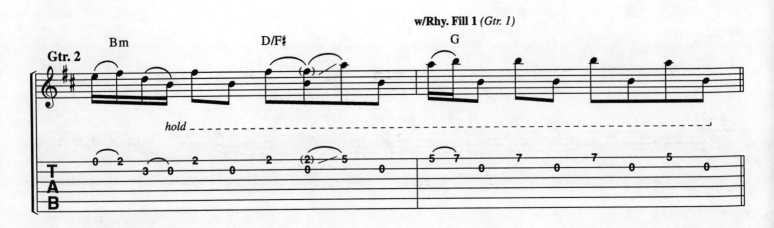

Pre-Chorus:
w/Rhy. Figs. 2 *(Gtr. 1, simile)* & 2A *(Gtr. 2)*

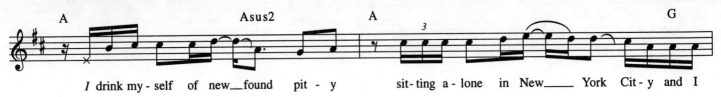

I drink my-self of new_found pit - y sit-ting a - lone in New_ York Cit - y and I

Chorus:
w/Rhy. Fig. 3 *(Gtrs. 1 & 2, 2 times)*

don't know why,_ don't know why._ So I walk *up* on_ high_

_ and I step to the_ edge_ to see my world_ be-low.

And I laugh *at* my - self_ while the tears roll_ down_

_ 'cause it's the world I_ know._ Oh, it's the world I_ know.

Verse 2:
Are we listening to hymns of offering?
Have we eyes to see that love is gathering?

Pre-Chorus:
All the words that I've been reading
Have now started the act of bleeding
Into one, into one.
(To Chorus:)

GUITAR TAB GLOSSARY **

TABLATURE EXPLANATION

READING TABLATURE: Tablature illustrates the six strings of the guitar. Notes and chords are indicated by the placement of fret numbers on a given string(s).

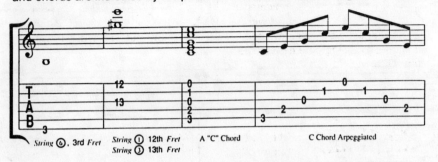

String ⑥, 3rd *Fret* String ① 12th *Fret* String ③ 13th *Fret* A "C" Chord C Chord Arpeggiated

BENDING NOTES

HALF STEP: Play the note and bend string one half step.*

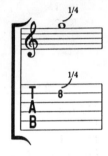

SLIGHT BEND (Microtone): Play the note and bend string slightly to the equivalent of half a fret.

BEND AND RELEASE: Play the note and gradually bend to the next pitch, then release to the original note. Only the first note is attacked.

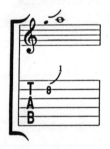

WHOLE STEP: Play the note and bend string one whole step.

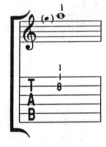

PREBEND (Ghost Bend): Bend to the specified note, before the string is picked.

BENDS INVOLVING MORE THAN ONE STRING: Play the note and bend string while playing an additional note (or notes) on another string(s). Upon release, relieve pressure from additional note(s), causing original note to sound alone.

WHOLE STEP AND A HALF: Play the note and bend string a whole step and a half.

PREBEND AND RELEASE: Bend the string, play it, then release to the original note.

BENDS INVOLVING STATIONARY NOTES: Play notes and bend lower pitch, then hold until release begins (indicated at the point where line becomes solid).

UNISON BEND: Play both notes and immediately bend the lower note to the same pitch as the higher note.

TWO STEPS: Play the note and bend string two whole steps.

REVERSE BEND: Play the already-bent string, then immediately drop it down to the fretted note.

DOUBLE NOTE BEND: Play both notes and immediately bend both strings simultaneously.

*A half step is the smallest interval in Western music; it is equal to one fret. A whole step equals two frets.

© 1990 Beam Me Up Music
c/o CPP/Belwin, Inc. Miami, Florida 33014
International Copyright Secured   Made in U.S.A.   All Rights Reserved

**By Kenn Chipkin and Aaron Stang

RHYTHM SLASHES

STRUM INDICATIONS: Strum with indicated rhythm.

The chord voicings are found on the first page of the transcription underneath the song title.

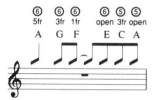

INDICATING SINGLE NOTES USING RHYTHM SLASHES: Very often single notes are incorporated into a rhythm part. The note name is indicated above the rhythm slash with a fret number and a string indication.

ARTICULATIONS

HAMMER ON: Play lower note, then "hammer on" to higher note with another finger. Only the first note is attacked.

LEFT HAND HAMMER: Hammer on the first note played on each string with the left hand.

PULL OFF: Play higher note, then "pull off" to lower note with another finger. Only the first note is attacked.

FRET-BOARD TAPPING: "Tap" onto the note indicated by + with a finger of the pick hand, then pull off to the following note held by the fret hand.

TAP SLIDE: Same as fretboard tapping, but the tapped note is slid randomly up the fretboard, then pulled off to the following note.

BEND AND TAP TECHNIQUE: Play note and bend to specified interval. While holding bend, tap onto note indicated.

LEGATO SLIDE: Play note and slide to the following note. (Only first note is attacked).

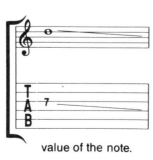

LONG GLISSANDO: Play note and slide in specified direction for the full value of the note.

SHORT GLISSANDO: Play note for its full value and slide in specified direction at the last possible moment.

PICK SLIDE: Slide the edge of the pick in specified direction across the length of the string(s).

MUTED STRINGS: A percussive sound is made by laying the fret hand across all six strings while pick hand strikes specified area (low, mid, high strings).

PALM MUTE: The note or notes are muted by the palm of the pick hand by lightly touching the string(s) near the bridge.

TREMOLO PICKING: The note or notes are picked as fast as possible.

TRILL: Hammer on and pull off consecutively and as fast as possible between the original note and the grace note.

ACCENT: Notes or chords are to be played with added emphasis.

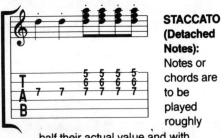

STACCATO (Detached Notes): Notes or chords are to be played roughly half their actual value and with separation.

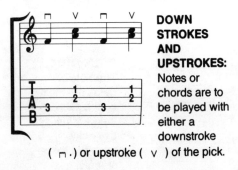

DOWN STROKES AND UPSTROKES: Notes or chords are to be played with either a downstroke (⊓ ·) or upstroke (∨) of the pick.

VIBRATO: The pitch of a note is varied by a rapid shaking of the fret hand finger, wrist, and forearm.

HARMONICS

NATURAL HARMONIC: A finger of the fret hand lightly touches the note or notes indicated in the tab and is played by the pick hand.

ARTIFICIAL HARMONIC: The first tab number is fretted, then the pick hand produces the harmonic by using a finger to lightly touch the same string at the second tab number (in parenthesis) and is then picked by another finger.

ARTIFICIAL "PINCH" HAR-MONIC: A note is fretted as indicated by the tab, then the pick hand produces the harmonic by squeezing the pick firmly while using the tip of the index finger in the pick attack. If parenthesis are found around the fretted note, it does not sound. No parenthesis means both the fretted note and A.H. are heard simultaneously.

TREMOLO BAR

SPECIFIED INTERVAL: The pitch of a note or chord is lowered to a specified interval and then may or may not return to the original pitch. The activity of the tremolo bar is graphically represented by peaks and valleys.

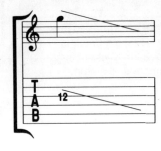

UN-SPECIFIED INTERVAL: The pitch of a note or a chord is lowered to an unspecified interval.